Arrest-Related Deaths Program: Data Quality Profile

Executive summary

The Arrest-Related Deaths (ARD) program is an annual national census of persons who die either during the process of arrest or while in the custody of state or local law enforcement personnel. The Bureau of Justice Statistics (BJS) implemented the ARD program in 2003 as part of the Deaths in Custody Reporting Program (DCRP). The DCRP was initiated to fulfill the data collection requirement of the Deaths in Custody Reporting Act of 2000 (DICRA, P.L. 106-247). It collects in-depth information on deaths during arrest and incarceration, and it provides national-level information on the deaths of suspects and offenders from their initial contact with law enforcement personnel through the time they are incarcerated in a jail or prison.

ARD data are collected to quantify and describe the circumstances surrounding civilian deaths that take place during an arrest or while in the custody of law enforcement. These data describe the prevalence and incidence of arrest-related deaths across the nation, identify the circumstances or activities that contribute to these deaths, and reveal trends in the causes and circumstances of these deaths in custody at national and state levels. These data can be used to inform specific policies that may increase the safety of law enforcement officers and citizens, identify training needs in law enforcement agencies, and assist in developing prevention strategies.

The current ARD program relies on state reporting coordinators (SRCs) in each of the 50 states and the District of Columbia to identify and report on all eligible cases of arrest-related deaths. BJS compiles data from the states to produce national-level statistics on deaths that occur in the process of arrest by, or while in the custody of, state and local law enforcement personnel. When the DICRA reporting requirements ended in 2006, BJS undertook efforts to understand the variability between SRCs, and within SRCs over time, in terms of data collection methodologies and available resources. This variability has led to concerns about definitions, data quality, and undercoverage error.

This report responds to issues with variability and profiles the data quality of the ARD component of the DCRP. The report (1) gives an overview of the ARD program, (2) describes the data collection methods used by SRCs, and (3) assesses the quality of the resulting data and coverage for eligible ARD cases that involve law enforcement homicides.

The variation in methodologies resulted in a significant underestimate of the annual number of arrest-related deaths, including both homicides by law enforcement officers and other types of civilian deaths. Key findings include—

- Nationally, the ARD program captured about 50% of the estimated law enforcement homicides during 2003–09 and 2011. This assessment did not examine the coverage of other deaths the ARD program is designed to capture, including those due to accidents, drug overdoses, and natural causes.

- The national coverage of homicides by law enforcement captured in the ARD program improved from 2003 through 2011. This was partially due to the use of open source searches to identify potential cases that were eligible for inclusion. Even with this improvement, assessments indicate that from 31% to 41% of the estimated homicides by law enforcement personnel were not captured in the 2011 ARD data collection.

- Significant challenges exist because of the lack of standardized modes for data collection, definitions, scope, participation, and the availability of resources.

1. Program overview

HIGHLIGHTS

- The Arrest-Related Deaths (ARD) program collects information on deaths occurring in the process of arrest.

- An arrest-related death is defined as any death (e.g., gunshot wound, cardiac arrest, or drowning) that occurs during an interaction with state or local law enforcement personnel, including those that occur—

  - during an attempted arrest or in the process of arrest

  - while the person is in law enforcement custody (before transfer to jail)

  - shortly after the person's freedom to leave is restricted.

- Exclusions include—

  - deaths of bystanders, hostages, and law enforcement personnel

  - deaths occurring during an interaction with federal law enforcement agents

  - deaths of wanted criminal suspects before police contact

  - deaths by vehicular pursuits without any direct police action.

1.1 Program purpose and justification

The Deaths in Custody Reporting Act of 2000 (DICRA; P.L. 106-297), signed into law on October 13, 2000, required that states applying for Violent Offender Incarceration/Truth-in-Sentencing (VOI/TIS) grants follow the U.S. Department of Justice guidelines for a quarterly data collection of inmate deaths from all state prisons (public and private), local jails, juvenile detention facilities, and police lockups, as well as deaths occurring in transit and in the process of arrest. Under DICRA, state applicants for VOI/TIS grants were required to provide assurance of

> "…reporting, on a quarterly basis, information regarding the death of any person who is in the process of arrest, is en route to be incarcerated, or is incarcerated at a municipal or county jail, State prison, or other local or State correctional facility (including any juvenile facility) that, at minimum, includes—

> - the name, sex, race, ethnicity, and age of the deceased

> - the date, time, and location of death

> - a brief description of the circumstances surrounding the death."

The Bureau of Justice Statistics (BJS) implemented the data collection requirement under DICRA legislation. In compliance with the specifications outlined in P.L. 106-297, BJS began quarterly data collections to cover all inmate deaths in local jails (2000), state prisons (2001), and juvenile correctional facilities (2002). In 2003, BJS expanded the Deaths in Custody Reporting Program (DCRP) to include deaths that occur in the process of arrest by state and local law enforcement agencies.

The DCRP provides data that describe the prevalence and incidence of deaths that occurred while the decedent was in the custody of law enforcement personnel, local jails, or state prisons. These data collections provide policymakers, public health officials, law enforcement officials, and correctional administrators with a comprehensive system for monitoring deaths within three major components of the criminal justice system: the police, local jails, and corrections. The DCRP collections are the only source of this type of information at national, state, and local levels.

Prior to the DCRP, prison mortality data were collected at the national level on a limited number of deaths (i.e., homicide, suicide, natural causes) and at levels of aggregation that precluded analysis of subpopulations. Jail mortality data were collected at infrequent intervals through BJS's *Census of Jails* series; however, like prison mortality data, these data were limited to broad categories of causes and provided limited information on the demographic characteristics of decedents. Deaths in juvenile correctional facilities were collected periodically by the Office of Juvenile Justice and Delinquency Prevention (https://www.ncjrs.gov/pdffiles1/ojjdp/228128.pdf). No national collection of arrest-related deaths, as described by the DICRA legislation, had ever been completed.[1] Arrest-related mortality data were restricted to small local studies, mostly at the agency level, and focused predominantly on officer-involved homicides (Klinger, 2012; Loftin, Wiersema, McDowall, & Dobrin, 2003).

With information collected through the DCRP, BJS can track changes in the mortality rates of persons who have contact with the police or are in custody in jail or prison. The DCRP data have improved our understanding of civilian deaths while in the criminal justice system. For example, through the DCRP, BJS has shown that almost 40% of deaths that occur in the process of arrest arise from causes other than officer-involved homicides of suspects (Mumola, 2007; Burch, 2011); that in any given year, about 80% of the roughly 3,000 jails in the United States have no deaths and, among those jails reporting deaths, the modal count is one death; that the leading cause of death in prisons is cancer, followed by heart disease; and that most inmates who died in custody had medical conditions that predated their arrival to prison or jail, as opposed to

---

[1] Two national-level programs, the Uniform Crime Reports–Supplementary Homicide Reports (SHR) and National Vital Statistics System (NVSS), collect information on homicides by law enforcement, but neither the SHR nor the NVSS captures the full scope of deaths specified by the DICRA legislation. The SHR data are limited to justifiable homicides by law enforcement. The NVSS data identify deaths attributed to legal intervention. Deaths that do not directly result from law enforcement action but still occur during the process of arrest (e.g., vehicular deaths resulting from pursuits, suspects dying from medical conditions, and suicides during standoff situations) are not identified in the NVSS as legal intervention deaths.

contracting a fatal disease while in custody (Noonan & Ginder, 2013). Since its initiation in 2003, the ARD program has released two reports on the number and characteristics of arrest-related deaths (Burch, 2011; Mumola, 2007).

In 2006, the DICRA reporting requirements expired. BJS continued to collect, analyze, and report on deaths in custody. In December 2014, the Death in Custody Reporting Act of 2013 was signed into law (P.L. 113-242, see https://www.congress.gov/bill/113th-congress/house-bill/1447/text).

1.2 Definitions

The DICRA legislation required states to submit quarterly data on deaths that occur in the process of arrest. BJS designed the ARD program's scope to include homicides, suicides, accidental deaths, and deaths attributed to intoxication and medical conditions that occur during a civilian interaction with state or local law enforcement.

BJS operationalized the DICRA term "arrest-related" to describe the range of circumstances pertaining to an arrest, including those that occur from the process of apprehension to detention. BJS defined a death as arrest related when the event causing the death (e.g., gunshot wound, cardiac arrest, or drowning) occurs during an interaction with state or local law enforcement personnel.[2] These events can be grouped into three categories: deaths that occur (1) while a person is detained or restricted and shortly after the person's freedom to leave is restricted, (2) during an attempted arrest or in the process of arrest, or (3) while the person is in custody (before transfer to jail). Exclusions to this definition are described in section 1.3.

Shortly after freedom to leave is restricted—All deaths that occur shortly after a person's freedom to leave is restricted by state or local law enforcement personnel should be reported to the ARD program if the circumstances causing the death occur during the interaction with law enforcement. For example, if a detained individual sustained an injury during an interaction with law enforcement personnel and died later as a result of those injuries, the death should be reported to the program.

Although the majority of deaths reported to the ARD program involve criminal suspects, individuals not considered subjects of arrest can be detained by law enforcement personnel, such as during a stop-and-frisk search or during a vehicle stop. In addition, individuals may be in the custody of law enforcement for medical or mental health assistance. Deaths of noncriminal persons that occur in the custody of state or local law enforcement personnel should be reported to the ARD

program when the deaths are attributed to events that occur while the person is engaged with law enforcement.

The most common types of noncriminal deaths reportable to the ARD program occur during law enforcement's response to service calls for assistance or transport. Often, these service calls are civilian requests for mental health or medical assistance. These incidents may involve individuals who are suicidal or displaying erratic behavior or may occur during transport to a mental health facility or hospital. Law enforcement may have engaged with the decedent to facilitate care during an emergency, assist with involuntary commitment to a medical facility, or support emergency medical technicians while transporting an individual for continued care.

During an attempted arrest or in the process of arrest— Arrest-related deaths include all deaths that occur during an interaction with law enforcement personnel in the process of arrest or attempted arrest, regardless of whether physical custody was established before the death. Deaths occurring before arrest include those that are attributed to events that transpired either during apprehension or while the decedent was detained for questioning or investigation.

Deaths that occur while law enforcement personnel attempt to apprehend or arrest an individual (e.g., those that occur during foot or vehicle pursuits of criminal suspects and during standoffs or barricade situations) are reportable. Common examples of deaths that occur during apprehension include officer-involved shootings; deaths related to the use of force or law enforcement compliance weapons[3] or tactics; vehicle accidents and collisions caused by either the decedent, intervening law enforcement personnel, or unrelated civilians; other types of fatal accidental injuries sustained while attempting to elude law enforcement personnel, such as falls from heights and drowning; and suicides committed during standoffs and barricade situations.

Deaths that occur during interviews and interrogations, or while a criminal suspect is detained for questioning or investigation, are also within the scope of the ARD program and should be reported. These arrest-related deaths may take place at a law enforcement facility or in the field. Examples of these types of deaths include those attributed to alcohol and drug intoxications, sudden medical conditions (e.g., cardiac arrest, asthma, stroke, or seizure), choking on ingested objects or other forms of asphyxiation, and suicides.

In addition to deaths that occur before a physical arrest, deaths that occur while law enforcement attempts to establish physical custody of a suspect are also reportable to the ARD program. All deaths that are attributed to weapon use by state or local law enforcement personnel are considered arrest related and are reported. Common examples of deaths attributed to law enforcement's use of weapons include officer-involved shootings, complications related to the use of conducted

---

[2]BJS collaborated with state and local law enforcement agencies and law enforcement professional organizations, such as the International Association of Chiefs of Police (IACP) and the National Sheriffs' Association (NSA), to establish the specific criteria for determining which deaths to include within the ARD program's scope. These callibrations addressed topics regarding which deaths should be eligible for reporting, the number and type of sources of existing data available in each state, and expectations for how states should identify within-scope deaths.

---

[3]Compliance or less-than-lethal weapons are designed to induce offender compliance while minimizing accidental, incidental, and correlative casualties associated with weapon use.

energy devices (i.e., Tasers or stun guns), accidents caused by the use of spike strips or other tire deflation devices, fatal injuries due to the use of impact devices (e.g., batons and soft projectiles) and complications due to the use of chemical agents(e.g., pepper spray and tear gas).

All deaths caused by law enforcement's use of restraint tactics are also reported to the ARD program. Eligible deaths attributed to restraint or use of other tactics include fatal injuries caused by physical fighting or struggle with law enforcement personnel; deaths caused by positional asphyxia or restraint in prone position; fatal injuries due to physical restraint by law enforcement personnel, such as those attributed to the use of control holds or neck restraint; and deaths caused by complications due to body compression.

While in custody (before transfer to jail)—Deaths that occur after law enforcement personnel have established physical custody of an arrestee are reported to the ARD program if the deaths occur while custody of the suspects resides with the arresting agency. These in-custody deaths can occur at the scene of the incident; during transport of a criminal suspect or transport of a person in need of medical or mental health assistance; or while a suspect is being held at a law enforcement facility, such as a booking center or lockup facility.

For the purposes of ARD, an in-custody death refers only to the deaths of criminal suspects under the control of state and local police officers and sheriffs' deputies during booking, but before arraignment or transfer to a jail or prison. Once an arrestee is arraigned or custody of the individual is transferred to a long-term correction facility, the death is no longer within the scope of the ARD program. The deaths of incarcerated inmates are recorded in either the jails or prisons component of the DCRP.

Common examples of deaths that occur during transport or confinement include those attributed to complications related to the use of weapons (e.g., a firearm or conducted energy device) during the arrest incident; injuries caused by the use of restraint or impact devices, as well as those resulting from physical altercation; fatal intoxications attributed to the overuse of alcohol and drugs; medical conditions; and suicides.

1.3 Exclusions

Not all deaths that occur during an interaction with state and local law enforcement personnel should be reported to the ARD program. Four general situations are typically excluded: (1) deaths of bystanders, hostages, and law enforcement personnel; (2) deaths of persons in the custody of federal law enforcement agents; (3) deaths of wanted criminal suspects before police contact; and (4) deaths by vehicular pursuits without any direct police action.

Deaths of bystanders, hostages, and law enforcement personnel—The deaths of innocent bystanders, hostages, and law enforcement personnel are excluded. Including persons killed in the course of law enforcement activities against whom no charges were intended was considered outside the scope of the ARD program.

Data on law enforcement personnel killed during interactions with civilians are outside the scope and are captured by the FBI in the Law Enforcement Officers Killed and Assaulted (LEOKA) collection.

Deaths by federal law enforcement—Deaths that occurred while the decedent was in the custody of federal law enforcement agencies (e.g., the FBI, Drug Enforcement Administration, or U.S. Marshals Service) are outside the scope of the ARD program as defined in the original DICRA, which did not apply to federal law enforcement agencies or the Federal Bureau of Prisons. Fatal incidents involving federal law enforcement personnel are reportable to ARD only if the interaction causing death also included state or local law enforcement personnel.[4]

Deaths of wanted criminal suspects before police contact—The death of a criminal suspect wanted by law enforcement personnel are not reported to the program if the death occurred before the decedent came into contact with law enforcement. The death of a person with an active arrest warrant are not reported to the ARD collection unless law enforcement personnel were present when the event causing the death occurred. If law enforcement personnel were actively attempting to apprehend a wanted suspect at the time the event causing the death occurred, the death is within the scope of the collection.

Deaths by vehicular pursuits without any direct police action—Although some vehicular deaths can be reported to the ARD program, those in which law enforcement did not take direct action against the subject or his or her vehicle should be excluded from the data collection. Cases in which a vehicular pursuit of an arrest subject involved direct action taken by law enforcement personnel against the subject, such as shooting at the subject's vehicle, ramming it, or otherwise forcing the vehicle to stop or leave the road (e.g., roadblocks or spike strips), are within the scope of the collection. Deaths resulting from vehicular pursuits—regardless of speed—are not reportable to the ARD program if the pursuit did not involve any direct law enforcement action taken against the subject and instead merely entailed following the subject.

---

[4] Current Death in Custody Reporting Act of 2013 (P.L. 113-242) includes federal law enforcement within scope.

2. Methodology

HIGHLIGHTS

- Centralized state reporting coordinators (SRCs) operate the state-level ARD data collection.

- The ARD program has three main tasks:
  - identify arrest-related deaths
  - acquire information about arrest-related deaths
  - submit the CJ-11 form, Quarterly Summary of Arrest-Related Deaths (or summary of incidents) and the CJ-11A form, Arrest-Related Death Report (or incident report).

- SRCs use one or more of the following sources to identify eligible ARD cases:
  - law enforcement
  - medical examiner or coroner
  - prosecutor's office
  - Uniform Crime Reports (UCRs)
  - National Violent Deaths Reporting System (NVDRS)
  - open-source media search.

To implement the ARD collection, BJS developed a program methodology that relied on establishing centralized SRCs and using them to operate state-level ARD data collections (see appendix B for a description of how the current ARD program methodology was developed).[5]

Since 2003, SRCs have been responsible for identifying all ARD reportable deaths in their states and for obtaining information about these deaths. BJS provided guidance in how to collect ARD data but did not require SRCs to use a specified, standard methodology. BJS recommends that states use one or more of the following procedures to identify arrest-related deaths: implementing legislation; contacting state medical examiner and county coroner officers; involving state and local prosecutors' offices; contacting the state police; expanding the role of the state UCR reporters; or conducting open-source searches.

Once a reportable death is identified, SRCs are directed to work with the law enforcement agency involved with the death to obtain the required data elements about the incident. When the SRC is unable to obtain full reporting from the law enforcement agency involved in the death, the SRC is asked to compile details of the event from official source documents

[5]When the DICRA legislation was enacted, only California and Texas had statutes requiring that information on arrest-related deaths be collected and reported at the state level. For the remaining 48 states and the District of Columbia, the ARD program was the first attempt to collect statewide counts of all deaths that occur in the process of arrest. In developing the program, BJS contacted multiple offices in each state to determine an appropriate reporting agent and data provider.

and to complete a CJ-11A Incident Report (appendix A). As a result, SRCs have developed strategies for identifying and collecting data that vary by the resources available to them. Consequently, the current ARD program design reflects many state-specific methodologies that are integrated into a single, national-level program.

2.1 Data providers

Information about data providers participating in the ARD program is available for calendar years 2003–11.[6] During 2011, 47 reporting offices submitted ARD data (table 2-1). Most States have maintained participating SRCs over time, with 36 states submitting ARD data every year of data collection since 2003 (states are not shown in table 2-1). Although a state may not have participated in the ARD program in a given year, arrest-related deaths may have been identified and reported by BJS staff in these states.

During 2011, a state criminal justice agency was the most common data reporting contact (16 states), followed by a department of public safety or other state law enforcement agency (14 states) (table 2-2). In three states, the department of corrections took a lead role in compiling ARD records.

Participation in the ARD program is voluntary without direct payment or compensation. Only SRCs employed by state justice statistics analysis centers (SACs) have received federal funds to support ARD-related work. SACs are units or agencies at the state government level that use information from all components of the criminal justice system to analyze statewide policy issues (see www.jrsa.org). SACs are maintained in various entities, such as state planning or coordinating agencies, governors' offices, criminal justice agencies, and universities.

For 32 states in 2011 (68%), the SRC office reporting ARD data also served as the SAC.

2.2 Data collection process

The ARD program data collection process includes three main tasks:

(1) identify arrest-related deaths

(2) acquire information about arrest-related deaths

(3) submit CJ-11summary of incidents and CJ-11A incident reports.

SRCs are responsible for identifying all arrest-related deaths within their states. Arrest-related deaths may be identified directly by the SRC or indirectly through assistance from another entity involved with the death (e.g., law enforcement agency) or death investigation (e.g., medical examiner's or coroner's office, prosecutor's office). SRCs use a variety of

[6]Although ARD data were accepted after 2011, program staff did not actively collect data for calendar years 2012 or 2013.

TABLE 2-1

States or jurisdictions that did not report to the Arrest-Related Deaths Program, 2003–11

State or jurisdiction	2003	2004	2005	2006	2007	2008	2009	2010	2011
Total reporting	44	46	46	44	47	43	42	47	47
Arkansas	/	■	■	■	■	/	/	/	/
District of Columbia	■	■	■	■	■	/	/	■	■
Georgia	/	/	/	/	/	/	/	/	/
Louisiana	/	■	■	■	■	■	■	■	■
Maryland	/	/	/	/	/	/	/	■	■
Mississippi	/	■	■	■	■	■	■	■	■
Montana	/	/	/	/	/	/	/	■	■
Nebraska	■	■	■	■	■	■	/	■	■
Nevada	■	/	/	/	/	■	■	■	■
New Mexico	■	■	■	■	■	/	/	■	■
North Carolina	■	■	■	/	■	■	■	■	■
Oklahoma	■	■	■	/	■	■	■	■	■
Tennessee	/	■	■	■	■	■	■	■	■
Wisconsin	■	■	■	■	■	/	/	/	/
Wyoming	■	/	/	/	/	/	/	/	/

Note: States not listed reported to the ARD program in each year from 2003 through 2011.
■Reported.
/ Not reported.
Source: Bureau of Justice Statistics, Arrest-Related Deaths Program, 2011.

TABLE 2-2.

Number of state reporting coordinators, by state, Statistical Analysis Center (SAC) status, and type of reporting office, 2011

Type of reporting office	Total	Located in SACs		Not located in SACs	
		Number	State	Number	State
Number of all reporting offices	47	32		15	
State criminal justice agency	16	14	AL, AZ, CT, DE, IL, IA, KS, KY, MT, NE, NY, RI, VA, WV	2	PA, VT
Department of public safety/law enforcement	14	9	CO, FL, MO, NJ, OH, OK, SC, SD, TN	5	DC, HI, MI, MN, WA
University	4	4	AK, MS, NV, NM	0	
Attorney general's office	4	2	CA, NH	2	ND, TX
Governor's office	3	3	MD, MA, UT	0	
State department of correction	3	0		3	ID, IN, LA
Office of the chief medical examiner	2	0		2	ME, NC
Office of public health	1	0		1	OR

Note: Four states did not report data in 2011.
Source: Bureau of Justice Statistics, Arrest-Related Deaths Program, 2011.

techniques to identify deaths that are consistent with ARD program definitions. BJS encourages SRCs to take an active approach in identifying deaths, rather than relying solely on a system of voluntary reporting by law enforcement or nongovernmental entities. Active strategies are those in which the SRC proactively searches for arrest-related deaths, such as methods that include surveying law enforcement agencies, mining existing data collections, and conducting regular open-source searches, in addition to possibly receiving voluntary submissions from law enforcement agencies and medical offices.

SRCs are responsible for obtaining complete incident reports for each arrest-related death in the state and for transmitting instruments to ARD program staff for data entry, analysis, and dissemination at the national level. Although all three of these components are incorporated into the national program design, the processes by which data are collected vary by SRC.

2.2.1 Active and passive approaches to case identification

In 2011, most SRCs employed active strategies for identifying deaths. Of the 45 SRCs reporting information about their data collection procedures, 41 reported using a proactive strategy to identify arrest-related deaths. The most common active identification strategy involved conducting open-source searches for reportable deaths. In total, 32 SRCs reported conducting web-based searches as a means for identifying reportable deaths: 16 conducted solely open-source searches, and 16 conducted open-source searches in addition to another strategy (table 2-3).

SRCs using passive methodologies rely on other agencies to identify arrest-related deaths. Passive strategies are those in which data are collected through voluntary submissions of completed CJ11A incident reports from other entities, such as law enforcement agencies and medical examiners' or coroners' offices. SRCs employing passive methodologies do not conduct independent searches for arrest-related deaths. SRCs in four states said that deaths were identified solely through voluntary reporting by law enforcement agencies.

TABLE 2-3

Number of states or jurisdictions using active case identification strategies, by data source, 2011

Source	Number
All states or jurisdictions	51
Active case identification strategies	41
Single-method identification	24
Open-source search	16
Law enforcement survey/referral	3
Medical examiner data request	3
Other[a]	2
Multiple-method identification	17
Open source and law enforcement survey/referral	7
Open source and database search[b]	5
Open source and medical examiner data request	4
Medical examiner and prosecutor survey	1
Passive case identification strategies	4
Unknown case identification strategies	2
Nonparticipating states	4

[a]Includes sole use of the National Violent Deaths Reporting System (one state) or reports to the office of the attorney general (one state).
[b]Includes National Incident-Based Reporting System (NIBRS), National Violent Deaths Reporting System (NVDRS), and Uniform Crime Reports (UCR).
Source: Bureau of Justice Statistics, Arrest-Related Deaths Program, 2011.

2.2.2 Number and type of case identification strategies

Of the 41 SRCs with known active case identification strategies, 17 mentioned using multiple strategies for identifying arrest-related deaths, while 24 (59%) said that they used a single method for identifying cases. Among those 24 SRCs, open-source searches were the most common (16 SRCs), followed by direct reporting by law enforcement agencies (3), a query of medical examiners' or coroners' databases (3), a query of the NVDRS (1), and officer-involved death reports submitted to the office of the attorney general (1).

The use of open-source searches as a method of identifying arrest-related deaths was also common among SRCs using multiple case identification strategies. Among the SRCs implementing multiple strategies for identifying deaths, 16 in 17 used open-source searches combined with other methods, such as surveys of law enforcement (7 SRCs) and queries of medical examiners' or coroners' databases (4 SRCs), NVDRS (3 SRCs), and the National Incident-Based Reporting System (NIBRS) or UCR (2 SRCs). One other SRC searched medical examiners' databases and conducted statewide surveys of prosecutors' reports.

2.2.3 Primary identification methodology

Of the 45 participating states with known case identification methodologies in 2011, 26 SRCs used the media and open-source searches as their primary manner of identifying arrest-related deaths (table 2-4).[7] Eight SRCs identified deaths primarily through direct reporting by law enforcement agencies, five through medical examiners' or coroners' offices, three through the NVDRS programs, two through the state attorney general's or prosecutors' offices, and one through the UCR program.

Although SRCs used similar strategies for identifying deaths, differences were found in how methodologies are applied. SRCs reported using media accounts as their primary case identification methodology more frequently than any other method; however, this strategy varied the most across states. For example, many SRCs stated that their methodology was to watch the local television news, read the newspaper, or both. Although some arrest-related deaths will be identified by monitoring local news, this method is not likely to be sufficient for identifying the full universe of reportable deaths. One problem relates to whether local outlets are capable of covering

[7]SRCs using multiple strategies for identifying arrest-related deaths were able to indicate which method was their primary method for collecting data and which strategy served as a secondary method for collecting data.

TABLE 2-4.
Primary case identification methodologies, 2011

Source	Number	Percent
All participating states or jurisdictions	45	100%
Open-source media search	26	58
Law enforcement agency report	8	18
Medical examiner database	5	11
National Violent Deaths Reporting System	3	7
State attorney general's or prosecutor's office	2	4
Uniform Crime Reports	1	2

Note: The primary source for identifying arrest-related deaths was unknown in two states. Four states did not report data in 2011.
Source: Bureau of Justice Statistics, Arrest-Related Deaths Program, 2011.

the ARD scope for the entire state, while another problem relates to whether this type of monitoring is conducted systematically. It was not clear from discussions with SRCs that routine procedures were employed when monitoring news outlets (e.g., daily monitoring or monitoring the same outlets). It was also unclear how SRCs determined which outlets to monitor and whether any investigation was conducted to assess the appropriateness or accuracy of the source content.

Besides traditional media, many SRCs also used open-source Internet searches to identify deaths. Although some specifically mentioned monitoring the web page of the state police for incidents of arrest-related deaths, others had a more difficult time specifying their procedures. Some SRCs also reported that they conducted searches for terms relating to arrest-related deaths, but it was unclear whether searches were conducted ad hoc or routinely. It was also unclear if the same terms were searched consistently or if SRCs varied their terms when searching for arrest-related deaths. Without information about specific search terms used by SRCs, the variation of search terms are unknown across SRCs. Overall, although 26 states reported using media searches as their primary mode for identifying arrest-related deaths, no two SRCs used the exact same procedures.

2.2.4 Types of state reporting coordinators and primary methods for identifying arrest-related deaths

SRCs were categorized by the location of their offices in an attempt to better understand whether there is a relationship between the type of reporting office and the primary method for identifying arrest-related deaths. Among the SRCs located in state criminal justice agencies, 10 in 14 relied on open-source searches as their primary method for identifying arrest-related deaths. Half (7) of the SRCs located in departments of public safety or another state law enforcement agency also used open-source searches as their primary means of identifying deaths. Among the 14 SRCs located in departments of public safety or another state law enforcement agency, three identified arrest-related deaths primarily through direct reporting by law enforcement agencies (table 2-5).

TABLE 2-5.
Primary information source for identifying arrest-related deaths, by location of state reporting coordinator office, 2011

Location of office	All offices	Open source search	Direct reporting by law enforce-ment	Data request to medical examiner or coroner	National Violent Death Reporting System	Investigative reports	Uniform Crime Reports
Total	45	26	8	5	3	2	1
State criminal justice agency	14	10	2	0	1	0	1
Dept. of public safety/law enforcement	14	7	3	3	0	1	0
University	4	3	1	0	0	0	0
Attorney general's office	4	1	2	0	0	1	0
Governor's office	3	1	0	1	1	0	0
Department of correction	3	3	0	0	0	0	0
Medical examiner's office	2	1	0	1	0	0	0
Office of public health	1	0	0	0	1	0	0

Note: The primary source for identifying arrest-related deaths was unknown in two states. Four states did not report data in 2011.
Source: Bureau of Justice Statistics, Arrest-Related Deaths Program, 2011.

2.2.5 Source of case information

Once an arrest-related death is identified, the SRC is responsible for either obtaining information about the death directly or coordinating efforts by other entities to obtain case-level information. In states in which SRCs identify reportable deaths, the SRC may take responsibility for acquiring information about the incident or may request that another agency involved with the death (e.g., law enforcement agency, medical examiner's office, or prosecutor's office) provide information about the circumstances surrounding the death. In states in which deaths are identified by other agencies, the agency that identified the death takes responsibility for gathering information.

SRCs responsible for directly obtaining information about the death acquire case information from a variety of sources, including police reports or press releases, death records or autopsy reports, legal accounts, and the media. Non-SRC entities responsible for gathering case information typically use the same data sources as SRCs because these agencies are often those responsible for initially collecting the information. For example, law enforcement agencies completing the CJ-11A will likely use information from the police reports they produced.

2.2.6 Overlap in sources used to identify deaths and to obtain case information

SRCs vary in the number and types of sources they use to obtain information about arrest-related death incidents. Some SRCs rely on a single source of information to both identify deaths and gather information about incidents. Other SRCs use a multistep data collection process in which information used to complete the CJ-11A comes from a source other than the one used to identify the death. For instance, a single-source data collection process could involve using a media account both to identify the arrest-related death and to obtain information about it. A multisource process involves using one source (e.g., media report) to identify a reportable death and one or more additional sources of information (e.g., a police report or autopsy report) to obtain case information.

Eleven SRCs (24%) used a single source of information for identifying arrest-related deaths and completing CJ-11A incident reports (figure 2-1). Of those, the most common source of information was law enforcement reports (six SRCs), followed by media reports (two SRCs), medical examiner records (two SRCs), and UCR data (one SRC).

Most SRCs (72%) relied on multiple sources of information to identify deaths and to obtain incident data during 2011. Thirty-six percent of SRCs relied on both the source of information used to identify arrest-related deaths and at

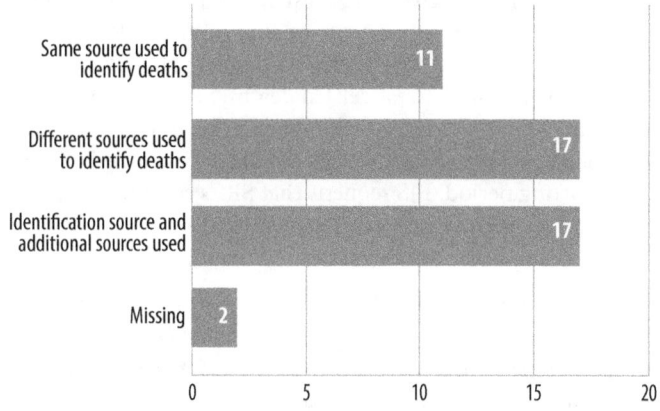

FIGURE 2-1

Overlap in sources used to identify deaths and to complete CJ-11A incident reports, 2011

Note: Four states did not report data in 2011.

Source: Bureau of Justice Statistics, Arrest-Related Deaths Program, 2011.

least one additional source to obtain the incident data for completing the CJ-11A. Thirty-six percent of SRCs used a multistep data collection process in which one source was used to identify deaths and a different source was used to obtain information about the death. The most common example of a multisource process involved using open-source searches to identify an arrest-related death and a police report to complete the CJ-11A.

During 2011, about two-thirds of SRCs used only official sources of information for obtaining data regarding incidents of arrest-related deaths (table 2-6). Law enforcement reports were the most common source of incident-level information about arrest-related deaths. A small number of SRCs (4%) relied on unofficial sources of information, such as journalistic accounts of events, to obtain details about reportable incidents.

TABLE 2-6.

Types of data sources used to obtain arrest-related death case information, 2011

Source	Number	Percent
Total state reporting coordinators	45	100%
Official sources data	30	67%
Law enforcement report only	19	42
Medical examiner report only	4	9
Multiple official sources	7	16
Combination of official and unofficial sources	13	29%
Unofficial sources of information	2	4%

Note: The primary source for identifying arrest-related deaths was unknown in two states. Four states did not report data in 2011.

Source: Bureau of Justice Statistics, Arrest-Related Deaths Program, 2011.

2.3 Completion of CJ-11 and CJ-11A instruments

The ARD program uses two data collection instruments, the CJ-11 Quarterly Summary of Arrest-Related Deaths (summary of incidents) and the CJ-11A Arrest-Related Death Report (incident report). The CJ-11 form is completed by SRCs and is a state-level count of arrest-related deaths. SRCs are directed to submit a CJ-11 form for each reporting period and to show a count of zero if no arrest-related deaths are identified within the reporting period. BJS requests that SRCs submit zero counts to distinguish between the measured absence of an identified death and missing data.

The CJ-11A form is a detailed incident report that describes the circumstances surrounding each reportable death. SRCs are asked to submit a complete CJ-11A incident report for each death recorded on the state-level CJ-11 summary form. Depending on the method used to identify the death and the agency responsible for acquiring information about the incident, the SRC may take responsibility for completing the CJ-11A forms or may request that another agency complete the forms.

Information about the entity responsible for completing CJ-11A forms during 2011 was available in 45 states. The law enforcement agency involved with the death was primarily responsible for completing CJ-11A incident reports in 20 states (44%) (figure 2-2). SRCs obtained case information and completed CJ-11A reports in 16 states (36%), followed by staff in medical examiners' offices (2 states) and prosecutors' offices (1 state). Multiple entities took responsibility for completing sections of the CJ11A incident report in six states, with joint efforts by the SRC and law enforcement agency in three states, the SRC and medical examiner's or coroner's office in two states, and the law enforcement agency and medical examiner's office in one state.

2.3.1 Data collection cycle

The ARD data collection is conducted on a calendar-year cycle. The program operates continuously and accepts submissions throughout the year. The ARD program also accepts reports of arrest-related deaths that occurred before the current calendar year and updates to previously reported data.

In January, BJS notifies SRCs that it is beginning a new year of ARD data collection and provides them with key program materials, including (1) the CJ-11 summary of incidents form, (2) the CJ-11A incident report, and (3) a question-by-question guide to aid in completing the CJ-11A (see appendix A for survey instruments and revisions to the CJ-11A incident report, 2003–13). In addition, BJS provides the SRCs with general information about the program, such as key dates, methods for submitting data, and contact information for ARD program staff.

When the DICRA legislation was in effect, SRCs were required to submit ARD data quarterly. They were asked to submit a CJ-11 Summary of incidents and corresponding CJ11A incident reports within 60 days of the end of the quarter. After DICRA expired in 2006, BJS relaxed the quarterly reporting requirement and gave SRCs the option of submitting their data either quarterly, annually, or on a schedule of their choosing. Of SRCs reporting ARD data in 2011, about half (49%) submitted data annually, while 28% continued to collect and report data quarterly (figure 2-3). Data can be submitted any time during the year, but SRCs must submit all annual CJ-11 and CJ-11A reports no later than March 1 of the following calendar year.

2.3.2 Data submission

After the SRCs complete their annual data collections, they transmit this state-level data to BJS for analysis. Historically, the ARD data collection was paper based. Data providers

FIGURE 2-2.
Entity responsible for completing CJ-11A incident reports, 2011

Number of states

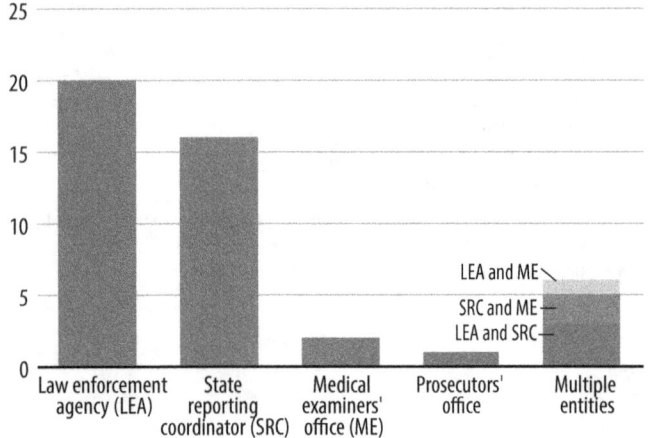

Note: The primary source for identifying arrest-related deaths was unknown in two states. Four states did not report data in 2011.
Source: Bureau of Justice Statistics, Arrest-Related Deaths Program, 2011.

FIGURE 2-3.
Arrest-related deaths data collection schedule, 2011

Percent

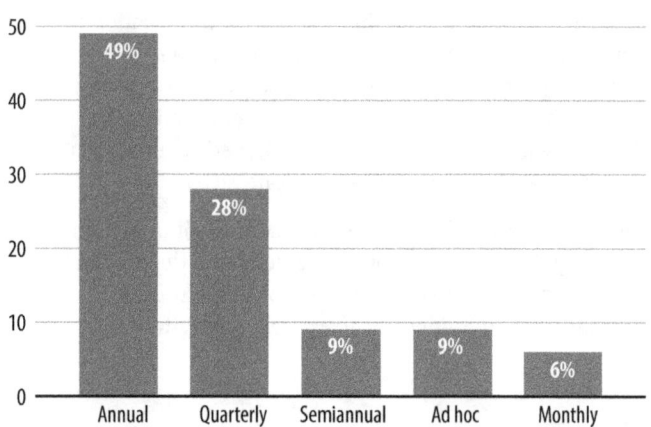

Note: Detail may not sum to total due to rounding. Four states did not report data in 2011.
Source: Bureau of Justice Statistics, Arrest-Related Deaths Program, 2011.

would complete paper versions of the CJ-11 and CJ-11A forms and mail or fax them to BJS. As the program developed, BJS began accepting the forms electronically through email. Electronic versions of the forms were submitted either as fillable PDFs or scanned documents. BJS staff would then enter information from the CJ-11A forms into a national database.

To improve efficiency, BJS established an Internet-based data collection tool for the ARD (see appendix B for a full description). This tool allows SRCs to enter CJ-11A information directly on a web-based reporting platform rather than transmitting the completed forms to BJS and its ARD program staff. Currently, ARD data can be submitted at any time and are accepted via postal mail, fax, or electronically through email, an uploaded PDF, or direct entry through the web-based reporting tool.

As noted previously, annual state-level ARD data are due by March 1 of the next calendar year. ARD staff review these data and assess them for completeness and consistency before entering them into the national database for analysis (see appendix C for a description of the BJS verification process). In addition, records are reviewed to determine whether each reported death falls within the ARD scope.

3. Program assessment

HIGHLIGHTS

- A national- and state-level comparison of ARD and SHR data collected 2003–05 showed that, despite convergence at the national level, there were considerable differences in ARD program coverage at the state level. Similar differences within states at the agency level were also found in an analysis of data reported to ARD and SHR in 2006–09.

- Nationally, the ARD program estimates that it has captured about 50% of all law enforcement homicides during 2003–09 and 2011.

- The national coverage of homicides by law enforcement that the ARD program captures improved from 2003 through 2011. Even with this improvement, assessments indicate that between 31% and 41% of homicides by law enforcement personnel were not captured in the 2011 ARD data.

The ARD program relies primarily on state-level respondents to gather and report information on deaths associated with the arrest process for all state and local law enforcement agencies. As described in the *Methodology* section (chapter 2), the manner in which these incidents are identified and subsequent information collected varies between and within states and over time, leading to nonsampling errors from differences in use and interpretation of definitions, scope, and data collection modes. Although an empirical assessment of the relative level of error associated with each data collection approach is not known and would be very difficult to design, many of these errors have been realized from internal audits and anecdotal

accounts from data providers and SRCs. Subsequently, this nonstandardized data collection process invites concerns about the coverage, bias, and reliability of reports.

This chapter describes critical aspects of the ARD data collection methodology, noting important limitations and challenges to producing valid and reliable national estimates. These challenges include variations in state-level methodologies related to (1) whether SRCs actively identify within-scope cases and the level of effort they apply to their search for reportable cases, (2) what SRCs use as their primary case identification strategies, (3) whether SRCs use one or multiple methods for identifying deaths, (4) what source of information they use to complete CJ-11A forms and whether they use multiple sources of information, and (5) which agency is responsible for completing the form. To highlight these challenges, we describe issues related to scope and definitions, to data collection strategies, and modes. We follow this description with an assessment of the coverage of the ARD program, focusing on law enforcement homicides.

3.1 Defining eligible incidents

The ARD program has definitions and a scope for eligible incidents that are difficult to consolidate into a comprehensive, precise set of terms. The program relies on a set of examples to help identify eligible cases and guide data collection agencies. An arrest-related death can occur at any time and in any location where law enforcement personnel and civilians interact, including while fleeing or being pursued, at scenes of arrest, at locations of medical or mental health assistance, and while the person is being transported to law enforcement or medical facilities or is detained at lockups or booking centers. The breadth of the ARD scope and the variety of circumstances and locations in which eligible deaths can occur make it difficult for state-level reporting agents to identify all reportable deaths.

3.1.1 Arrest-related

The term "arrest-related" in the DICRA legislation encompasses a variety of circumstances from the process of apprehension to detention. Confusion about the program scope arose from the expansive nature of the terms "in the process of arrest" and "arrest-related." For example, in the law enforcement community, "the process of arrest" means Mirandizing and handcuffing suspects and is not used to describe pursuits, officer-involved shootings, or other uses of force. However, for ARD purposes, arrest-related deaths can occur before, during, or after an arrest, as long as the event that causes the death occurs during an interaction with state or local law enforcement personnel. An arrest-related death describes deaths caused by law enforcement personnel, and those attributed to suicide, intoxication, accidental injury, and medical emergencies or health complications. The resulting characterization of arrest-related deaths is more inclusive than a collection of officer-involved shootings or justifiable homicides by law enforcement, which may be more easily understood as eligible incidents. The breadth of the program's definition of "arrest-related" creates problems in identifying eligible cases, likely contributing to a significant undercount of incidents.

3.1.2 Custody

The term "custody" includes physically touching or putting hands on an arrestee. For the ARD program, it also includes any act that indicates an intention to gain control of an arrest subject under the authority of the law or any situation in which a person's freedom to leave is restricted by state or local law enforcement personnel. This includes deaths occurring while law enforcement officers actively pursue or attempt to apprehend persons of interest or criminal suspects, regardless of whether physical custody is established. For example, many ARD cases are officer-involved shootings, and virtually none of these incidents involved subjects who were already in the physical custody of law enforcement personnel.

Custody includes individuals in physical custody of law enforcement without being in the process of arrest. To gain control of a situation, law enforcement personnel sometimes handcuff or detain persons against whom they do not plan to file charges (e.g., mentally ill or intoxicated persons, or others who pose a danger to their own safety).

3.1.3 Reporting deaths in jails

The goal of the DCRP is to identify and record all deaths of civilians in contact with law enforcement and correctional personnel. BJS implemented three separate data collection systems to capture deaths occurring in the process of arrest and those that occur while the person is detained in jail or prison. Deaths reportable to the ARD program are limited to those that occurred while the decedents were in the custody of law enforcement. Therefore, deaths that occur after an individual has been processed and custody has been transferred to a holding facility are outside the ARD scope. Given that the functions of some law enforcement agencies include detention, some SRCs reported difficulty in determining whether the decedent died in the custody of law enforcement or the custody of a correctional facility.

3.2 Assessment of data collection modes

3.2.1 Standardization

The ARD program has implemented variable methodologies since its first collection in 2003. As a result, data providers have designed and developed state-level data collections according to their preferences, their capabilities, and the resources available to them. The flexibility of the ARD data collection allows state-level data providers to use a variety of data sources and to rely on those that are most reliable in their particular states, but it presents significant challenges for collecting

statistically sound, national-level data because of the variability in data quality both within and across states. BJS has developed standardized data collection instruments (CJ-11A form), training materials, working definitions, and a web tool to assist SRCs in gathering and submitting the ARD information (see Appendix B). However, significant challenges within and between states exist in terms of mode, source, and quality.

3.2.2 Variation in program methodologies across states

SRCs developed their data collection methodologies in relation to their preferences and resources. As a result, the ARD program operations varied among participating states (see chapter 2: *Methodology*). Deaths may be identified from one or more resources from among media, open sources, law enforcement agencies, and medical examiners' or coroners' offices. The information sources consulted for completing each CJ-11A form also differed, and included media reports, police reports, medical examiner or coroner reports, case reports from the division of criminal information, or any combination of these sources. Data collection methodologies also differed by the agency responsible for completing the CJ-11A form, which can include the SRC, a law enforcement agency, a medical examiner's or coroner's office, or a combination of those offices.

BJS assessed the SRCs' primary method for identifying deaths, the sources of information used to complete the CJ-11A incident report, and the entity completing the CJ-11A. BJS determined that SRCs used a wide range of methods for collecting ARD data in 2011. The most common method (nine SRCs) for collecting ARD data was for the SRC to identify cases through open-source searches.[8] Then, the SRC asked the law enforcement agency involved with the death to complete a CJ-11A incident report using the agency's official data about the case. The second most common method (six SRCs) for collecting ARD data was direct reporting by the law enforcement agency involved with the death. In these states, the law enforcement agency involved with the arrest-related death took responsibility for identifying it, obtaining and completing a CJ-11A incident report using the agency's official data, and submitting the form to the SRC. In three states, SRCs identified deaths through media searches and completed CJ-11A instruments by obtaining the manner and cause of death from a medical examiner's or coroner's office. The rest of the information requested on the CJ-11A form was obtained through the same open-source record used to identify the death, namely, media accounts of events. Two SRCs identified arrest-related deaths through open-source searches and completed the corresponding CJ-11A instruments with information obtained in the media account used to identify the death. The remaining 24 states reporting information about their 2011 ARD data identification and collection strategies used unique methodologies with varying combinations of the source used to identify the arrest-related death, the agency

---

[8]The open-source search methodology is a general description for review of publicly available data. This term does not indicate a specific or single procedure or strategy for identifying and collecting data.

responsible for completing the CJ-11A form, and the source of information for completing the CJ-11A form.

Most states (26) relied solely on open-source searches to identify ARD-eligible cases. Although about half of the participating states said that they used open-source searches as their primary strategy for identifying deaths, no standard methodology exists for this type of identification procedure. Therefore, each of these 26 states was likely to use different mechanisms, searches, and monitoring plans for identifying arrest-related deaths.

3.2.3 Variation in program methodologies within states

Some SRCs noted that they did not have a standard operating procedure for identifying or collecting information on arrest-related deaths. They could specify the primary strategies they used to identify cases (e.g., media or law enforcement) and whether or not they also used alternative methodologies for identifying deaths. However, the SRCs suggested that it was more difficult to describe their exact data collection procedures because they often varied from one case to another. For example, SRCs relying on media or open-source searches described identifying cases by a variety of means. These included watching television, reading local newspapers, using Google Alerts to conduct daily web-based searches of key words or phrases, monitoring the state police web page, and searching other websites. In discussions with SRCs, it appeared to be more common for deaths to be identified ad hoc rather than through specified, standard procedures conducted routinely. Of the SRCs reporting more standardized procedures for identifying cases, some said that their methods of obtaining the data needed to complete the CJ-11A varied from case to case. For instance, some states that relied on law enforcement agencies to complete the CJ11A forms had contingency plans for collecting data if the law enforcement agency involved with the death refused to supply the information. One SRC reported that only about 50% of law enforcement agencies return the completed CJ-11A form. When the law enforcement agency failed to provide the completed form, the SRC attempted to obtain a report from the medical examiner's office for the information they needed to complete the form. If the information required to complete the CJ-11A was unavailable from the medical examiner's office, the SRC used media reports to complete the report.

Data collection methodolgies for SRCs participating in the ARD program differed over time. A survey of SRCs conducted in 2007 revealed that 42 of 47 that reported data used more than one source of data to identify deaths and complete CJ-11A forms. Commonly referenced sources included local law enforcement agencies (43 SRCs), media (30), medical examiners' or coroners' offices (23), state police (19), state UCR/SHR reporters (9), and state attorneys general or prosecutors (6). A follow-up discussion conducted in 2012 suggested that 28 of the 46 states reporting data used a single source of information for identifying cases. Of these, commonly referenced single sources of information

included media (16 SRCs), law enforcement agencies (7), medical examiners' or coroners' offices (3), the state attorney general or prosecutor (1), and the state NVDRS reporter (1). Twenty of the 46 SRCs reporting data indicated that they used multiple sources of information to complete CJ-11A forms for identified deaths (16 used two sources, and 4 used three or more sources). As a result of the variability both within and between states, records were often identified through a variety of means and comprised both official and unofficial accounts of the events.

3.3 Assessment of data quality and coverage

Given the concern about the lack of standardization both across and within SRCs in terms of data collection modes, definitions, scope, and availability of the necessary resources, BJS assessed the quality of the program's coverage—that is, how well the program performs in capturing the full universe of eligible arrest-related deaths.

3.3.1 2003–05 national and state assessment

Initial efforts began in 2007 with a focus on assessing the coverage of the 2003–05 ARD program by comparing homicides reported to ARD with those reported in the Supplementary Homicide Report (SHR) (Mumola, 2007). The SHR is a component of the FBI's Uniform Crime Reporting (UCR) program, which compiles information on crimes known to state and local law enforcement agencies in the United States. While the UCR provides aggregate annual counts of the number of homicides occurring in the United States, the SHR data provide additional information about each homicide incident, including the jurisdiction, month, year, and circumstances associated with the incident. Like the ARD, the SHR data have limitations. Most notably, the SHR program is voluntary, so a number of law enforcement agencies either do not consistently send their data to the SHR or do not submit it at all.[9] The SHR, however, represents the only other national database that can provide sufficient information on the circumstances surrounding law enforcement homicides to allow comparison with the ARD program.[10]

The ARD-SHR comparisons were limited to law enforcement homicides because, unlike the ARD program, the SHR does not record law enforcement-involved deaths that are attributed to suicide, intoxications, accidental injury, or natural causes. Also unlike the ARD program, the SHR includes only those homicides by law enforcement in which the use of force was ruled justifiable. Deaths due to unjustified use of lethal force by law enforcement personnel are counted with other murders

---

[9]See *The Nation's Two Measures of Homicide*. NCJ 246832, BJS web, September 2014.

[10]The NVSS is a national database that captures homicides occurring in the United States, but it does not link homicides that are arrest-related with specific law enforcement agencies as the SHR program does. This link to a law enforcement agency is critical for capturing-recapturing the analytic approach used to assess the ARD coverage.

and cannot be disaggregated for comparison to ARD. The ARD counts of homicide by law enforcement include all deaths that result from the use of force.

Results of this assessment indicate that, nationally, a similar number of officer-involved homicides were recorded in the ARD and SHR programs. In the aggregate, the two programs collected very similar counts from 2003 through 2005, with 1,095 homicides recorded in ARD and 1,082 justifiable homicides recorded in the SHR. However, the aggregated, national-level comparison of the ARD and SHR data masked differences in reporting at the state level.

Similarly, the aggregate analysis at the state level likely also masked differences within states at the agency level. In most states, the ARD and SHR counts of law enforcement homicides showed small differences in the number of deaths reported to each program, but because arrest-related deaths are rare events, even small differences in state-level counts could result in a substantial change in the proportion of reported deaths. In 33 states, the two measures differed by fewer than 10 deaths from 2003 through 2005. Nine states reported counts that differed by at least 20 deaths, with the difference ranging from 22 to 194 homicides. California—one of 2 states with a statute requiring that all arrest-related deaths be reported to the state attorney general's office—had the largest reporting variation, with 354 justifiable homicides by law enforcement reported to the SHR from 2003 through 2005 but less than half as many (160) reported to the ARD program. Over the same period, Florida reported 98 law enforcement homicides to the ARD program but did not report any data to the SHR. Taking the higher count reported by each state for each year yields a total of 1,489 reported law enforcement homicides from 2003 through 2005—more than a third as many as those reported to either program.

3.3.2 2006–09 agency assessment

BJS conducted an agency-level analysis of homicides by law enforcement reported to the ARD program and to the SHR for 2006–09 to determine the number of cases recorded in the SHR that were not recorded in ARD and vice versa. Homicides were disaggregated by agency for this comparison, using the agency's originating identification (ORI) number. Law enforcement agencies were matched across data sources, and the numbers of recorded homicides were compared to better understand how the coverage issues identified in the state-level analysis were affected by variation in reporting by law enforcement agencies. BJS was interested in determining whether the differences in reporting were due to (1) different agencies reporting to each system or (2) the same agencies reporting different counts to both systems.

BJS conducted this analysis by creating overage variables to represent the number of additional cases reported to the ARD program and to the SHR by each law enforcement agency. For example, if the Springfield Police Department reported one homicide by law enforcement to ARD and three homicides by law enforcement to the SHR, the ARD overage variable would equal 0 and the SHR overage variable would equal 2. Although this analysis was limited in that it did not determine whether the one case reported to ARD was also one of the three cases captured in the SHR, it was able to provide evidence of at least two homicides by the Springfield Police Department that were not captured in ARD. The SHR overage homicides were summed as an indication of the minimum number of homicides by law enforcement missing from ARD (identified as ARD missing). Similarly, the ARD overage cases were transformed into SHR missing. For the Springfield Police Department, the ARD missing equaled 2.

This procedure was conducted for every law enforcement agency that reported a homicide by law enforcement to either ARD or the SHR from 2006 through 2009. The analysis resulted in a minimum of 701 cases reported to the SHR that were not recorded in ARD, and a minimum of 935 cases that were recorded in ARD, that were not captured in the SHR. Although this analysis was limited by several factors—namely, that the data were not disaggregated by year of death or characteristics of the decedent—it demonstrated coverage error at the agency level.

3.3.3 2003–11 individual case assessment

To better understand the source of discrepancies in reporting across the ARD program and the SHR, BJS compared individual-level homicide records in each collection. For this assessment, BJS examined law enforcement homicides in ARD and compared them with justifiable homicides in SHR using the data available from the entire ARD program and a capture-recapture analysis.[11] This analysis addresses a key obstacle to understanding the coverage of the ARD program. Because the ARD program includes only state and local law enforcement agencies that have been involved in one or more identified arrest-related deaths and does not include agencies that did not have an identified arrest-related death, it is difficult to make inferences about coverage using ARD data alone. Because the SHR data also provide incident-level information on homicides, they can be used to help assess the coverage of the ARD data collection. The assessment consisted primarily of matching records from the two programs and determining the amount of overlap between collections to estimate the total universe of reporting deaths. Similar to the other assessments using SHR data, this assessment is limited to justifiable homicides by law enforcement (see *Arrest-Related Deaths: Technical Report*, NCJ 248544, BJS web, March 2015).

Under the current ARD collection method, SRCs identify deaths, then usually contact the local agencies in which the deaths occurred to get the information they need to complete a CJ-11A for each death. By this method, BJS can affirm that an identified death occurred and met the criteria to be included in ARD, but it cannot confirm that there were in fact no other

---

[11]ARD data are available for program years 2003–09 and 2011. However, the ARD program is designed to capture all arrest-related deaths, including those due to accidents, drug overdoses, and natural causes. These incidents are not assessed in this analysis.

arrest-related deaths. This is because BJS does not survey each of the approximately 18,000 state and local law enforcement agencies in the United States to determine whether arrest-related deaths occurred.

By linking records submitted to the ARD and SHR collections, it is possible to make inferences about the total size of the officer-involved homicide population and, therefore, about the population coverage achieved in the ARD program. This analytical technique, known as capture-recapture, is typified by studies of wild animal populations, although it is widely used in the study of human populations as well, particularly in coverage evaluations for censuses. The ARD coverage assessment is based on traditional capture-recapture methods, but unique characteristics of ARD data necessitate special techniques, including probabilistic record linkage between data sources and adjustments for unobserved agencies.

3.3.4 Probabilistic case-level linking

Capture-recapture analysis depends on the ability to link records across data sources. In wildlife applications, this requirement is easily met as captured animals are identified through tagging. In the context of a coverage assessment using an auxiliary data source not collected as part of the study, this requirement becomes more difficult. Because decedents are not uniquely identified across data sources (e.g., by name or Social Security number), record linkage must be based on comparable decedent demographic and incident characteristics. As linkages made without unique identifiers are inherently uncertain, decedents are matched between ARD and SHR sources probabilistically on the basis of measured similarity between records, within a monte carlo replication framework. This means that although a given ARD decedent will be linked to either no SHR decedents or a single SHR decedent in a particular replicate, the nature of the link for that ARD decedent (i.e., whether it is linked and, if so, to which SHR decedent) is allowed to vary across replicates according to the probabilities associated with particular record pairings, on the basis of measured similarity between cases. Probabilistic linking is random in nature and incorporates additional uncertainty into the process of estimating population coverage. Monte carlo replication allows for this additional uncertainty to be captured in variance estimates.

3.3.5 Capture-recapture analytic approach

Once decedent records have been linked across the ARD and SHR, capture-recapture methods can be used to estimate the total law enforcement homicide population and the proportion of that population covered by the ARD program. This analysis makes use of the commonly applied Lincoln-Petersen (LP) estimator, with modifications for bias amelioration necessitated by the characteristics of the ARD program (Seber 1982).

The simple LP method assumes that law enforcement agencies that were not recorded in the ARD data did not have any officer-involved homicides during the observation period. This approach provides the highest possible ARD coverage estimate and the lowest estimate of the total population of law enforcement homicides because it assumes that the data are representative of agencies with true zero counts rather than missing responses. Essentially, the simple LP approach presents a best case scenario for estimating the ARD coverage rate.

The adjusted LP estimate assumes that a portion of the law enforcement agencies that did not report to the ARD program did have homicides and that they had, on average, the same number of officer-involved homicides as law enforcement agencies that reported data to the program. The adjusted approach assumes that some law enforcement agencies with homicides are unrecorded in the ARD data and that these agencies represent a random sample of the overall set of agencies with homicides.

3.3.6 Results

Following the simple LP approach, the estimated ARD coverage of all law enforcement homicides is 49%, with a 95% confidence interval ranging from 47% to 50%. In other words, the ARD program captured only about half of all law enforcement homicides in the United States during the observation period. The adjusted LP approach, the ARD program is estimated to capture 36% of all law enforcement homicides, with a 95% confidence interval ranging from 35% to 38%. Therefore, the coverage of law enforcement homicides captured in ARD could be as low as 35% or as high as 50%. These results indicate that the ARD program may provide a slightly higher coverage of homicides by law enforcement than the SHR, which is estimated to cover 46% of officer-involved homicides at best. Further analysis of the data suggests that about 28% of homicides by U.S. law enforcement agencies are not captured by either the ARD or SHR programs. Overall, these findings indicate serious deficiencies in the ability of the ARD program, as well as the SHR, to capture a universe of reportable homicides by law enforcement.

Despite these deficiencies, coverage of these deaths has improved since the inception of the program. Differences in state participation (see table 2-1) and changes in state-level methodologies contribute to national variation in annual coverage rates. Despite dips in coverage in 2005 and 2008, results from both the simple LP and the adjusted LP approaches indicate that ARD coverage of law enforcement homicides has increased over time, with the most pronounced improvement occurring in the most recent years of data collection (figure 3-1).

FIGURE 3-1.

Proportion of law enforcement homicide universe covered by ARD, by estimation method, 2003–09 and 2011

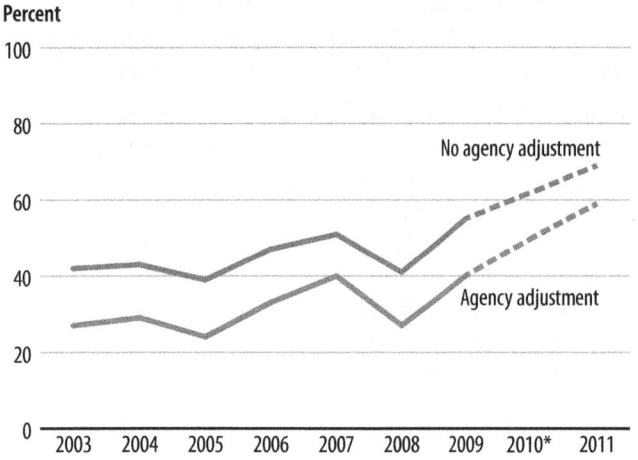

*Data are not shown for 2010 due to an incomplete data collection.
Source: Bureau of Justice Statistics, Arrest-Related Deaths Program, 2011.

During 2003, the first year of data collection, the estimated coverage of homicides by law enforcement was from about 27% (adjusted LP) to 42% (simple LP). Except for data collected in 2008, the coverage of law enforcement homicides captured in ARD improved from 2006 through 2011.[12] Using the simple LP approach, the ARD coverage of officer-involved homicides grew from 51% in 2007 to 55% in 2009 and 69% in 2011. The adjusted LP estimate (worst case coverage scenario) for 2011 (59%) indicated better coverage than the simple LP estimate (best case coverage scenario) for 2009 (55%).

These data indicate that the data collection methods used in more recent years are associated with better coverage of law enforcement homicides. This conclusion is supported by the fact that the adjusted LP approach also demonstrates improved coverage over time, growing from 40% in 2007 and 2009 to 59% in 2011. The gap between the adjusted and unadjusted coverage estimates narrowed by 2011, a further indication of improved methodologies. Even with this improvement, between 31% and 41% of actual homicides by law enforcement personnel were not captured in the 2011 ARD data.

---

[12]The 2010 ARD data were not included in the capture-recapture work.

The assessment is not without limitations. Conducting capture-recapture approaches at the state level was determined to be not statistically sound, given the relatively low number of cases reported to the ARD and SHR programs during 2011. For example, four states (Delaware, Rhode Island, Vermont, and Wyoming) had zero homicides by law enforcement recorded in either ARD or the SHR. As such, it was not possible to estimate the coverage rate of homicides by law enforcement using simple and adjusted LP approaches at the state level.

4. Conclusion

HIGHLIGHTS

- Significant challenges exist with the lack of a standardized mode for data collection, definitions, scope, agency participation, and the availability of resources.

- The current findings are consistent with prior studies that have shown considerable variation from state to state and over time in reporting to one national system or another.

- BJS may provide more prescriptive guidance or requirements regarding identifying cases and collecting data, but should also incorporate the differences between states in the availability of reliable sources for information on arrest-related deaths.

- When choosing solutions for a complete and accurate data collection, BJS should consider ways to standardize the data collection process, implement mandatory reporting by law enforcement agencies, dedicate resources and funding to support data collection efforts at the state and local levels, and focus on a more restricted definition and scope of eligible cases.

The ARD program is designed to be a national census of civilian deaths when the event causing the death occurs during an interaction with state or local law enforcement. Understanding when law enforcement officers are involved in a situation in which a community member dies during an arrest is critical to a democratic society (Fyfe 1981, 2002; McEwen, 1996; Klinger, 2008). BJS designed the ARD data collection methodology to rely on reporting from independent state reporting coordinators (SRCs). The manner in which ARD data are collected varies from state to state and often depends on the resources available to SRCs. This variability in approaches has led to questions about whether these data collection methodologies are capable of capturing the universe of arrest-related deaths and of law enforcement homicides in particular.

Previous research has explored the utility of the Supplementary Homicide Report (SHR), the National Vital Statistics System (NVSS), law enforcement agency records, media reports, and the ARD program for providing reliable statistics on the number of law enforcement homicides in the United States. This body of literature has generally concluded that there is no single, reliable system either for reporting or accessing data about arrest-related deaths; no one system consistently outperforms others. Furthermore, comparison of various data sources at the national level masks significant variations in reporting to one source or another at the state and jurisdiction levels (Loftin et al., 2003; Mumola, 2007; Sherman & Langworthy, 1979).

The current ARD methodology summarized in the *Methodology* section (chapter 2) and the results of the capture-recapture analysis described in the *Program Assessment* section (chapter 3) echo the conclusions of this body of research and highlight the continuing obstacles to collecting valid and reliable information about arrest-related deaths. At best, the ARD program captured approximately half of the estimated law enforcement homicides in the United States during 2003–09 and 2011. Consistent with other research on the utility of existing sources of data regarding arrest-related deaths, we found that the current data collection process results in a significant underestimation and potentially a biased picture of arrest-related deaths in the United States (Borrego, 2011; Ho et al., 2009). Some evidence indicates that the system's coverage has improved over time. Considering the 2011 data alone, the ARD program was estimated to capture as many as 69% of all law enforcement homicides in the United States, up from capturing 42% in 2003.

Although no current national-level system sufficiently measures all arrest-related deaths in the United States, previous research has shown that one system captures more cases than another in some states but not in others (e.g., Loftin et al., 2003; Mumola, 2007). Some evidence also indicates that using data from a combination of systems will result in better coverage. The current analysis found that the ARD program covered approximately half of the estimated law enforcement homicides in the United States during 2003–09 and 2011, but combining data from the SHR and the ARD increased coverage to 72%. To improve ARD coverage of arrest-related deaths, the ARD program might therefore build on two aspects of the current design to (1) allow some variation in the methods used to identify cases from state to state and (2) require that multiple data sources be used to compile information about arrest-related deaths within each state.

First, variation in the methods used to identify arrest-related deaths and collect information about them might be warranted from state to state, depending on the resources available within that state. The source that captures more arrest-related deaths varies from state to state, which should not be ignored when developing a more robust ARD data collection system.

Second, most SRCs employed a methodology that combines information from multiple sources. Given the limitations of existing national-, state-, and local-level data systems, combining data from all available systems should provide a more comprehensive picture of arrest-related deaths. Identifying cases from multiple systems will require significant resources to ensure that reports are not duplicated. Further,

timeliness and availability are an issue. Many datasets are not available in the current year and may lag multiple years behind other sources. Relying on multiple systems would also require an SRC who has access to and who systematically reviews all the relevant systems.

A survey that collects information about arrest-related deaths directly from local law enforcement agencies (rather than through the SRCs) provides an additional option for improving ARD program coverage. However, this method would require significant resources.

To achieve any improvements in coverage and consistency in reporting, the ARD program needs more prescriptive guidance or requirements on how arrest-related deaths are identified and report them to BJS. Currently, BJS provides definitions, examples, and general guidance on how SRCs might go about identifying arrest-related deaths and reporting information about them, but it does not require that SRCs follow a specific methodology. Furthermore, case identification and data collection methodology in each state is largely determined and driven by the individual SRC's own experience and available resources. Applying consistent definitions and systematic means of identifying deaths and collecting information about them from all appropriate sources in the jurisdiction is critical to improving ARD program coverage.

The scope of the current ARD program may also contribute to underreporting. The analyses reported in the *Program Assessment* (chapter 3) and cases found in the SHR and NVSS are limited to law enforcement homicides. The ARD program is designed to capture all arrest-related deaths, including those due to accidents, drug overdoses, and natural causes. It is the only system that attempts to collect these data, and it could provide critical information on cases that are missing or underreported in other sources, such as deaths following the use of tactics commonly referred to as less than lethal, including Tasers and restraint procedures. However, arrest-related deaths other than law enforcement homicides can be difficult for SRCs to define and identify from the sources available to them. Furthermore, the more clearly defined law enforcement homicide type of arrest-related death still suffers from significant undercoverage, as shown in the capture-recapture analyses presented in chapter 3. Improvements to the ARD program might be realized by first focusing solely on law enforcement homicides. After the data collection methodology has been defined, made routine, and shown to result in sufficient coverage for law enforcement homicides, a more expansive definition of arrest-related deaths might be explored.

BJS should consider ways to standardize the data collection methodologies to improve the reliability and validity of capturing eligible cases and overall data quality.

References

Borrego, A. (2011). Arrest-related deaths in the United States: An assessment of the current measurement. Master's degree thesis, Arizona State University. http://repository.asu.edu/attachments/56537/content/Borrego_asu_0010N_10572.pdf

Burch, A. (2011). Arrest-related deaths, 2003–2009–statistical tables. (NCJ 235385). Washington, DC: Bureau of Justice Statistics. Retrieved from http://www.bjs.gov/content/pub/pdf/ard0309st.pdf

Fyfe, J. (1981). Observations on police deadly force. *Crime & Delinquency, 27*, 376–389.

Fyfe, J. (2002). Too many missing cases: Holes in our knowledge about police use of force. *Justice Research and Policy, 4*, 87–102.

Ho, J.D., Heegaard, W.G., Dawes, D.M., Natarajan, S., Reardon, R.F., & Miner, J.R. (2009). Unexpected arrest-related deaths in America: 12 months of open source surveillance. *Western Journal of Emergency Medicine, 10*(2), 68–73.

Klinger, D.A. (2008). On the importance of sound measures of forceful police actions. *Criminology and Public Policy, 7*, 605–617.

Klinger, D.A. (2012). On the problems and promise of research on lethal police violence: A research note. *Homicide Studies, 16*, 78–96.

Loftin, C., Wiersema, B., McDowall, D., & Dobrin, A. (2003). Underreporting of justifiable homicides committed by police officers in the United States, 1976–1998. *American Journal of Public Health, 93*(7), 1117–1121.

McEwen, T. (1996). National data collection on police use of force. (NCJ 160113). Washington, DC: Bureau of Justice Statistics. Retrieved from http://www.bjs.gov/content/pub/pdf/ndcopuof.pdf

Mumola, C.J. (2007). Arrest-related deaths in the United States, 2003–2005. (NCJ 219534). Washington, DC: Bureau of Justice Statistics. Retrieved from http://bjs.ojp.usdoj.gov/index.cfm?ty=pbdetail&iid=379

Noonan. M.E., & Ginder, S. (2013). Mortality in local jails and state prisons, 2000–2011–statistical tables. (NCJ 242186). Washington, DC: Bureau of Justice Statistics. Retrieved from http://www.bjs.gov/content/pub/pdf/mljsp0011.pdf

Seber, G.A.F. 1982. The estimation of animal abundance and related parameters. Macmillan Publishing, New York, New York, USA.

Sherman, L.W., & Langworthy, R.H. (1979). Measuring homicide by police officers. *Journal of Criminal Law and Criminology, 70*, 546–560.

Appendix A

Tracking deaths in "the process of arrest" by state and local law enforcement presented a wide array of circumstances that are difficult to capture. To establish a standardized reporting form and process, in 2002 the Bureau of Justice Statistics (BJS) began working with states and law enforcement professional organizations to develop preliminary questionnaires. The process yielded two data collection forms, the CJ-11 Quarterly Summary of Deaths in Law Enforcement Custody (commonly called the summary of incidents form) and the CJ-11A Addendum, Law Enforcement Custodial Death Report (commonly called the incident report) (http://www.bjs.gov/index.cfm?ty=dcdetail&iid=428#Questionnaires).

The CJ-11 summary of incidents form was to serve as a quarterly summary of arrest-related deaths occurring in each state disaggregated by sex. In addition, the CJ-11 provided instructions for submitting data, examples of reportable deaths, and descriptions of the types of deaths that should be excluded from the data collection. State reporting coordinators (SRCs) were asked to submit a completed CJ-11 form indicating their statewide count of reportable deaths for each quarter of the calendar year. SRCs were instructed to complete a CJ-11 form with a count of zero if no arrest-related deaths were identified in the state. BJS used these forms to determine state participation in the Arrest-Related Deaths (ARD) program. SRCs were instructed to report zero counts to distinguish between the measured absence of an identified death and missing data.

On the CJ-11A incident report, SRCs were asked to describe the circumstances surrounding each arrest-related death they listed on the summary of incidents form, detailing one death per CJ-11A form. The 2003 CJ-11A form comprised 13 items to be completed for each death and an additional set of 5 items for those deaths that occurred before booking (A1–A5) or a set of 4 items for deaths that occurred after booking (B1–B4). It included items about the decedent, such as his or her name, date of birth, sex, and race/Hispanic origin. It featured questions regarding the manner and cause of death and asked whether the cause of death had been determined by a medical examiner or coroner. The CJ-11A also captured information about the decedent's interaction with law enforcement (i.e., the name and originating identification [ORI] number of the law enforcement agency involved, location of the event, whether charges had been filed against the decedent, and the most serious offense with which the decedent was being charged at the time of death) and whether the death occurred before or after booking.

For arrest-related deaths that occur before booking, SRCs were instructed to complete Section A of the CJ-11A form. Section A included additional items about the incident between law enforcement and the decedent, including whether the decedent sustained fatal injuries during the event, and if so, how the injuries were sustained; whether the decedent was restrained in the time leading up to the death, and if so, the type of restraints devices were used by law enforcement; and the decedent's behavior during the interaction with law enforcement (i.e., appeared intoxicated, threatened officers, resisted being handcuffed or arrested, tried to escape or flee, physically fight with the officers involved, or used a weapon to threaten or assault officers). Section A also included items regarding the type of weapon that caused the death and the type of location where the decedent expired (e.g., crime or arrest scene, medical facility, or en route to booking center).

SRCs were instructed to complete Section B of the CJ-11A form for instances in which the death occurred after booking while the decedent was being held in a temporary holding facility (but before arraignment transfer to a long-term correctional facility). Section B included items on when the decedent was booked into the law enforcement facility (i.e., date and time of entry) and the decedent's condition at the time of booking (e.g., appeared intoxicated, exhibited mental health problems, or exhibited medical problems). Section B also included information about who caused the death (i.e., deceased, other detainees, or law enforcement or correctional staff) for deaths attributed to homicide and accidental injury and the means of death (e.g., firearm, blunt instrument, cutting instrument, strangulation, or intoxication) for nonnatural deaths.

Revisions to the instruments

BJS has continued to evaluate the CJ-11 and CJ-11A since the instruments were implemented in 2003. The content of the CJ-11 summary form has remained relatively stable. A national listing of SRCs was added to the CJ-11 in 2005 and remained until 2013, when it was transferred to the CJ-11A incident report. The CJ-11 summary report was updated in 2013 to include revised reporting instructions and the option to complete the form as an annual summary (in addition to the continued use of reporting quarterly information). In addition, SRCs were no longer required to disaggregate state-level summary counts by sex.

The CJ-11A incident report has undergone several revisions since the original version. The first revision to the instrument was in 2007, which were minor and included (a) removing "stun gun or Taser" as a response to "What type of weapon(s) caused the death?" and (b) adding "conducted energy device (e.g., Taser or stun-gun)" as a response to the type of restraint device used in the time leading up to the death or the events causing the death. In 2008, a response of "No – medical/mental health assistance call" was added as a response to "Had charges been filed against the deceased at the time of death?" In addition, a response of "Pepper spray, mace" was added as a response to the type of restraint device used in the time leading up to the death or the events causing the death. Finally, "conducted energy device" was added back to the responses categories for "What type of weapon(s) caused the death?"

More significant chances to the CJ-11A instrument occurred in 2009, when the title of the instrument changed from "Deaths in Custody – Law Enforcement Custodial Death Report" to the "Arrest-Related Death Report." This change was made to help clear up confusion about the scope of the program. Even among law enforcement agencies providing data to the ARD program, the "deaths in custody" terminology led some to assume officer-involved shootings are not reportable because in the vast majority of cases, the decedent is not in the physical custody of law enforcement. The shift to the term "arrest-related" was intended to describe the wider scope of deaths reportable to the program.

In addition to the title change, the 2009 CJ-11A was structurally changed to remove the designation between sub-sections A and B. Before 2009, agencies completed either Section A or Section B depending on whether the death occurred before or after booking. Beginning with the 2009 version of the CJ-11A, respondents were asked to complete the items formerly in Section A for all reportable deaths. If the death occurred after to booking, respondents were asked to also complete all items formerly in Section A in addition to the items formerly found in Section B. While this change did not affect reporting for deaths occurring before booking, information on events that took place during the arrest were now required for deaths occurring post-booking.

Other changes to the 2009 CJ-11A included adding responses to preexisting items and adding an item on the decedents' use of weapons during the event. A notable addition to the 2009 instrument was the inclusion of "exhibit any mental health problem" as a response to indicate the decedent's behavior during the incident. Other additions to the form included a response category for injuries inflicted by law enforcement officers during transit or booking and widening the scope of the decedent's behavior during the incident to include certain attempted actions. For example, previous versions of the instrument asked respondents to indicate whether the decedent grabbed, hit, or fought with law enforcement officers, where the 2009 version sought to also include attempted physical altercations with law enforcement.

While the majority of the content remained the same, modifications were made to the 2010 CJ-11A. Some changes included a shift in focus from obtaining knowledge about whether or not "a medical examiner or coroner conducted an evaluation to determine the official cause of death," to whether or not the information about the decedent's manner and cause of death supplied on the CJ-11A were determined from documents created by a medical examiner or coroner. In addition, "alcohol/drug intoxication" was added as a response to whether the deceased died from a medical condition or from injuries sustained during the arrest process. Other changes included adding "firearm discharge" as a device used by law enforcement during the arrest process and adding "don't know" as a response option for questions.

In 2010, BJS held a meeting of experts to review of the ARD collection and solicit feedback on the data CJ-11A form. Participants in this meeting included law enforcement personnel, medical examiners and coroners, SRCs, and researchers in the law enforcement and public health fields. The ARD CJ-11A incident report was revised in 2012 in light of comments received from the meeting. The revised 2013 CJ-11A instrument was pilot tested in June 2012 with nine of the program's current SRCs.

In June 2012, BJS asked nine of the program's current SRCs to assess the revised instrument and related instructions in terms of substance, breadth, and clarity. Specifically, BJS asked the SRCs to evaluate whether the questionnaire items enhanced the quality, utility, and precision of the information to be collected and to note any items that were unclear, concerns with respect to the availability of the information requested, and response burden. Lastly, SRCs were asked to complete the revised version of the CJ-11A form for a death record that was previously submitted to the ARD program.

BJS removed items that required respondents to speculate about outcomes or that relied on respondents' opinions or perceptions. For example, BJS removed items related to alleged criminal involvement in the events leading up to the death, removed an item that had asked respondents to indicate whether the decedent "appeared intoxicated" or "exhibited mental health problems." BJS removed other items that were repetitive or could be determined from responses to other items. For example, Item 13 in the old instrument ("Did the deceased die from a medical condition, injuries sustained during the arrest process, or alcohol/drug intoxication?") was omitted because this information could be determined from information provided in response to tem 9 ("What was the cause of death?"). In addition, four questions about deaths occurring at a booking center or police lockup were omitted because the items either asked for speculative information or were redundant.

Before revision, the CJ-11A did not have reporting instructions or a national list of SRCs, both of which were included only on the CJ-11 summary of incidents form. The revised CJ-11A instrument includes a description of what deaths should be reported, contact information for assistance in completing the form, instructions about how to submit the completed form, and contact information for each SRC. The revised CJ-11A also includes a "data supplied by" section to assist SRCs in tracking where the information about each death is coming from.

BJS changed the order of items on the revised CJ-11A to improve the flow of the instrument. Items were reorganized into groups that reflect characteristics of the incident, characteristics of the decedent and actions the decedent took during the interaction, actions of law enforcement personnel during the interaction, and characteristics of the death. The structure of questions changed from a "Mark all that apply" format to a "yes/no" format to improve the quality of the data. Forcing those filling out the form to reply to each response category lessens the risk that people will skip over responses that should have been marked. In addition, after the pilot test, BJS removed an item regarding whether the decedent had a history of mental illness out of concern that the information obtained from this question would not be reliable.

Appendix B

A fully integrated web portal was to enhance the Arrest-Related Deaths (ARD) program data collection process by centralizing efforts to communicate the purpose and goals of the program. The web portal (www.bjsard.org) consists of both a public website for communicating information about the ARD program and a private online data entry and case management system that is available to state reporting coordinators (SRCs). The ARD portal provides users with a centralized location for accessing program information, such as background information, a flier for distribution to law enforcement agencies, an explanation of program-related terms, responses to frequently asked questions, program policies and announcements, arrest-related deaths publications, CJ-11 and CJ-11A data collection instruments, and on-demand training webinars.

The main benefit of the web portal is that it reduces the time it takes to enter ARD data and gives the ARD project team greater control over the reporting process. The ARD portal contains a private and secure section where SRCs can submit their CJ-11 and CJ-11A data. It allows SRCs to directly enter CJ-11A information on a web-based reporting tool (WRT) rather than having to obtain completed forms and transmit them to the ARD program staff. Before the launch of the WRT, ARD program staff would receive data from SRCs and enter it into a national database.

The WRT ensures that SRCs are using the correct CJ-11A form based on the year of the incident, which is a level of control that cannot be obtained when using hardcopy forms. For example, respondents in some states routinely report data on older, outdated CJ-11A forms. Requiring SRCs to use the WRT minimizes their use of outdated forms because the online forms are updated automatically.

When using the WRT, SRCs can monitor, review, edit, and approve their submissions before the data are deemed final in the system, which is useful when SRCs receive updated case information. SRCs may have to track an arrest-related death for a long time before they have all the relevant information to officially submit the case. Once a case is entered, it remains in the user's list of cases and the SRC can add to the record as information becomes available. The WRT facilitates cleaner data entry because it increases efficiency in data collection by reducing the need for post-entry editing and review.

The WRT contains a back-of-the-house validation code to ensure that the initial submission is as accurate as possible. Specifically, as the SRC enters a case the WRT will notify the SRC of inconsistencies in the data and require that the SRC address them before final submission. For example, if the SRC indicates that a weapon was used but did not specify what type of weapon, the WRT will display a message telling the user to specify the type of weapon before the WRT will move to the next item. The WRT also allows help text to be embedded next to each question to guide the SRCs when they are filling out the form.

The WRT's audit function tracks when changes are made to submitted data and who made the changes. It can also track information such as the time lapse time between initial entry of the case and completed verification. This audit history enables the Bureau of Justice Statistics to electronically compare an original data submission to the final case record.

The WRT also improves data security. Submitting the ARD data via the WRT increases the security of that data by encrypting the web session using Secure Socket Layers (SSL). SSL technology is an improvement over the former method of sending files as email attachments that may or may not have been encrypted. Logistical problems, such as mailbox size limitations, are also reduced. SRCs also can upload data files to the ARD web portal in a secure fashion.

Appendix C

Description of BJS's data verification process

State reporting coordinators (SRCs) submit their state's incident-level data (CJ-11A forms) to the Bureau of Justice Statistics (BJS) for national-level analysis. BJS staff review them for completeness and internal consistency before entering them into a national database.

If a CJ-11A report has missing information and responses that appear to be inconsistent or inaccurate, BJS staff take steps to complete or reconcile the information. Records are considered inconsistent or inaccurate if a response to one CJ-11A item contradicts a response to another item on the form. For example, a CJ-11A form might have a cause of death listed as "gunfire" but indicate that no weapons were used during the incident.

In other cases, discrepancies in reporting may be identified across an SRC's records, suggesting that coding procedures were not uniform. For example, deaths in which the manner was coded as "accidental alcohol/drug intoxication" and the cause of death coded as "overdose" could have a variety of responses to "Did the deceased die from a medical condition or from injuries sustained during the arrest process?" Those responses might include (1) medical condition only, (2) injuries only, (3) both medical condition and injuries, and (4) don't know.

If missing information and apparent inconsistences are discovered, BJS staff try to obtain additional case information to supplement the data, both by filling in missing data and verifying the validity of responses. Staff use the decedent's name and the name of the law enforcement agency involved in the death to conduct open-source searches. These searches yield information from media reports, law enforcement press releases, autopsy reports or death evaluations, and legal proceedings. Staff use these sources to supplement missing data and to correct inconsistent or contradictory information on CJ-11A forms. All modifications to submitted CJ-11A forms are noted in a Microsoft Word document, along with explanations for changes, and then sent to SRCs for verification.

During this verification process, BJS prepares a status report. The status report (1) serves as a receipt listing every name recorded in the collection for each SRC, (2) indicates whether each case submitted is complete or incomplete, (3) identifies cases that are out-of-scope, and (4) identifies cases that are within-scope that the SRC did not submit.

Status reports contain the names of all decedents recorded in each annual collection to confirm that BJS received all the data the SRCs submitted and ensure that BJS staff and the SRCs agree on who is included in the data. In addition, this list is an avenue through which BJS educates SRCs about any data submitted that were out-of-scope and data that were not identified through the SRC's methodology.

These reports also indicate whether BJS considers each case to be complete or incomplete. BJS records a case as complete if every item on the CJ-11A has a response and if the responses are internally consistent. If all responses are entered on the CJ-11A, but one or more responses are not consistent (or do not make logical sense) when considered with other item responses, the record is classified as incomplete. If BJS determines a record is complete, the status report will indicate (1) the name of decedent, (2) the date of death, and (3) that the record is complete and data will be recorded in the national database as originally submitted.

BJS considers records as incomplete if there are missing data or if there are inconsistences across the submitted responses. In addition to recording the decedent's name and date of death, the status report will also indicate the specific items that have missing or inconsistent data. In some instances, BJS will mark a record as incomplete to note a change made to the data. BJS makes an effort to explain why changes were made to data to improve the standardization and quality of future data.

Another example of missing data occurs when CJ-11A forms lack the manner and cause of death. This information is often left out because the autopsy report or death certificate was not available when the record was submitted. In these cases, BJS follows up with the SRCs at the end of the data collection cycle to determine if updated information is available. Cases are recorded as incomplete if responses seem logically inconsistent.

The status reports also indicate records that were submitted by the SRC and excluded from the collection by BJS. The most common reason cases are excluded is because the record has already been recorded in the Deaths in Custody Reporting Program (DCRP) – Jails data collection. BJS checks all Arrest-Related Deaths (ARD) program records against other DCRP collections to identify duplication across programs. If a death is reported to both ARD and one of the correctional components of the DCRP, the case remains in the DCRP Jails or Prisons collections and is excluded from ARD. BJS uses a hierarchy which specifies that duplicate cases submitted to the DCRP should be retained as correctional (i.e., DCRP Jails or Prisons) cases because presence in one of the correctional components indicates that custody of the decedent was transferred from law enforcement at some point.

Lastly, the status report notifies SRCs of reportable deaths identified by ARD program staff that were not included in the SRC's submission. In the process of obtaining additional information on the cases submitted, BJS staff may identify arrest-related deaths referenced in the open-source materials. For example, a journalistic account of the death of one arrestee might note that it was the law enforcement agency's third officer-involved death of the year and recount the circumstances surrounding the two previous deaths. BJS staff would then check the records submitted for the two additional deaths. If an identified death had been previously submitted by the SRC, BJS staff would not take additional steps beyond verifying that the information provided on the CJ-11A was correct. If an identified death has not been previously submitted, staff will note the name of the decedent, the law enforcement agency involved with the death, and the date or month of death on the status report. When possible, BJS provides SRCs with additional information about the cases the SRC missed, such as a copy of the law enforcement press release or legal proceedings. SRCs are asked to follow up on newly identified cases to confirm that they are eligible for inclusion in the program, and if eligible, complete a CJ-11A incident report.

BJS follows up with the SRC to improve the quality of the data submitted and the standardization of future program data. Concentrated follow-up with SRCs regarding the quality of the data submitted occurs during the summer. SRCs are reminded to submit their responses to issues identified on the status report and to submit any additional cases they may have identified after their initial submission of data. All follow-up contact with the SRCs typically occurs via email. SRCs may respond to status reports in whatever format is easiest for them, and ARD program staff will modify the previously submitted CJ-11A forms as needed. Follow-up contact for SRCs who did not submit their state's ARD data begins 60 days after the end of the year. These respondents receive emails asking them to submit their data from the prior calendar year as soon as possible.

The ARD data verification process was automated in 2012. ARD staff developed a codebook for standardizing state-level data submissions, which was tested for inter-rater reliability before being implemented. A SAS-based programming code was written to conduct missing, error, range, and consistency checks on data submitted by SRCs. Beginning with the 2011 collection, data were reviewed and a machine-edit process conducted a random review of records to check for data entry errors. This process is based on a series of checks, guided by the ARD codebook, that review and flag potentially erroneous data. Flagged cases are then exported to an Excel file for review by BJS staff.

Paradata

In preparing the status reports, BJS identifies common sources of reporting errors both across and within SRCs' reports. BJS began documenting reporting errors in 2010 while processing the 2007–09 data to better understand data quality issues. BJS used the 2007–09 data to create state-level narratives that indicated the number of (1) records submitted by the SRC, (2) submitted out-of-scope records excluded during BJS's verification procedures, and (3) within-scope records identified by BJS independent of what was submitted by SRCs.

In addition, BJS categorized all identified arrest-related deaths by the manner and cause of death (e.g., homicide by law enforcement—gunshot, or suicide—asphyxiation), and whether specific records had information missing or inconsistent responses (and the CJ-11A item number in which problems were identified). These SRC assessments also indicated the manner and cause of deaths identified solely by BJS through open-source searches to determine whether there was a pattern in the types of cases BJS was able to identify through open-source searches. In addition, BJS staff collected information on whether the case could be found online using the data the SRC submitted, through searches of the decedent's name and the name of the law enforcement agency involved with the death.

The results of these initial assessments indicated that SRCs were coding data inconsistently both within and across SRC agencies. Inconsistencies in responses were related to more complex manners and causes of death. Data contained discrepancies when the manner and cause of death appeared to contradict each other. For example, a medical examiner or coroner might rule the manner of death as a homicide and list the cause of death as cardiac arrest—a cause that might intuitively be associated with illness or natural causes. In these instances, SRCs indicated problems with completing CJ-11A items that pertained to whether the deceased died from a medical condition or from injuries sustained during the event, how the injuries were sustained (e.g., inflicted by law enforcement, self-inflicted—accidental, or not applicable), and whether a weapon caused the death. These types of deaths were often associated with the use of a stun gun or Taser during the interaction with law enforcement personnel or events that involved foot pursuits and physical struggles or altercations.

Other CJ-11A discrepancies were related to items indicating whether or not charges had been filed against the deceased at the time of death and, if so, which offenses were the most serious offenses being charged. Variation in criminal codes across states contributed to inconsistencies in reporting information. However, more significant issues were caused by inconsistent interpretations of the items on the CJ-11A form related to potential charges. Some CJ-11A records contained information about the reason for the interaction with law enforcement, such as a citizen-initiated call for service or an unlawful action observed by law enforcement. Other records contained only information about illegal activities that occurred during the interaction and provided no insight as to why or how the decedent came into contact with law enforcement personnel.

Although these records may have indicated the initial reason for the interaction (which may have not been criminal), many failed to capture criminal behaviors that transpired during the event. The most common source of error was the failure to include assaults against law enforcement personnel during the interaction with the decedent. During BJS's verification process, staff identified a number of records that did not include actions taken by the decedent against law enforcement personnel such as physical altercations, assaults with weapons, attempted murders, and homicides of law enforcement. SRCs were inconsistent both within and across states when completing information related to expected charges. This finding was especially pronounced when the initial reason for the law enforcement–decedent interaction was attributed to a request for service regarding mental health assistance.

In looking at the 2007–09 data, it became clear that SRCs were not applying consistent program definitions to cases when determining whether they were eligible for reporting. SRCs were reporting deaths outside of the ARD program scope, as well as failing to identify eligible deaths. In addition, the analysis of the paradata indicated that specific CJ-11A items were more problematic than others, and that certain types of arrest-related deaths also contributed higher levels of reporting error.

BJS took additional steps to quantify reporting error in 2010. ARD staff began collecting information about the records submitted by SRCs that included the date each CJ-11A was received by BJS, the date each form was entered, and the entity that identified the death (i.e., solely identified by the SRC, independently identified by both the SRC and BJS, or solely identified by BJS). In 2011, ARD staff expanded the paradata to include the date and reason for contacting the SRC, the date when a change was made to the data submitted, the name of the person who modified the data submitted, and the reason the data were changed.

BJS identification methods

Independent of the SRCs' efforts to identify ARD-reportable deaths, BJS began to monitor open sources for arrest-related deaths in January 2010. BJS staff identify within-scope deaths by using Google Alerts and by monitoring websites. Google Alerts are email updates of the latest relevant Google results based on queries established by the user to monitor the web for specific terms. BJS established a Google Gmail account for the ARD program and specified the words that Google should look for. The Google Alert system then searches media outlets nationwide and compiles relevant articles into an email for each specified term. The ARD email account receives daily emails that alert BJS when the specified search terms are used in the title of an article or news story.

Staff look through the alert emails to determine if an arrest-related death was captured in an article identified by Google. Each alert email may contain a series of articles, some containing accounts of within scope deaths. For example, an alert for the term "standoff" can yield 30 articles; of those, three articles may contain accounts of an arrest-related death. If an arrest-related death is identified through the Google Alerts, BJS will save the media accounts of the incident and forward the information to the SRC in the state where the death occurred. At that point, the SRC takes responsibility for verifying that the death is reportable and for obtaining a complete CJ-11A incident report. Depending on the timing

of the arrest-related death incident and on the SRC's data submission schedule, CJ-11As for deaths identified by BJS may be received at the same time as the other arrest-related deaths in the state or the information may be received independently at a later point in time.

BJS also monitors websites to identify deaths. These websites contain information supplied by the public about deaths that occur during interactions with law enforcement personnel. BJS monitors TNT – Truth Not Tasers (http://truthnottasers. blogspot.com/), a website that lists the names of individuals that died after an alleged shock from a conducted energy device. One of its pages, "A list of the dead," contains the decedent's names, age, date of death, and city of death. BJS compares this list to data submitted by SRCs to determine whether there are names on the TNT list that were not reported to the ARD program. If a previously unreported death is identified using the TNT list, BJS will seek additional information about the incident to better assess whether the death is reportable to program. Similar to the Google Alerts procedures, staff will forward information about the event to SRCs and the SRC will take responsibility for verifying the inclusion of the death in the program and obtaining a complete CJ-11A incident report.

Other websites used by BJS to identify arrest-related deaths include the Wikipedia page "List of killings by law enforcement officers in the United States" (http://en.wikipedia.org/wiki/ List_of_killings_by_law_enforcement_officers_in_the_ United_States,_August_2012). This website contains "lists of people killed by nonmilitary law enforcement officers, whether in the line of duty or not, and regardless of reason or method." The Wikipedia list contains the decedent's name, age, date of death, city and state of death, and a brief description of the event. The website also links a media account of the event as the reference for the information provided. BJS also monitors Cops Shooting People (http://copsshootingpeople.wordpress. com/) and Civilians Down (http://civiliansdown.com/site/ #sthash.Er0FGjOZ.dpbs).

BJS also routinely monitors the Officer Down Memorial Page (ODMP), a web-based list of law enforcement officers who have died. Although the deaths of law enforcement officers is outside of the scope of the ARD program, the ODMP website is monitored to identify instances in which civilians and officers both die during an interaction. For example, the ODMP website indicates that 12 officers died as a result of vehicular assault during 2011. The perpetrators of two of the assaults also died during the interaction and were within scope of the ARD program.